READABOUT
Wheels

Text: Henry Pluckrose
Photography: Chris Fairclough

W
FRANKLIN WATTS
LONDON • NEW YORK • SYDNEY

What do you need
to make this bike work?

What happens to the wheels when you push the pedals?

Wheels are made in many sizes.

All wheels are the
same shape.
You could not have a
square wheel
or one shaped like a triangle.

The centre of a wheel
is called the hub.
A wheel turns on an axle.
The axle fits into the hub.

The hub is joined
to the circular rim —
sometimes by thin spokes
and sometimes by thick
pieces of wood or metal.

Some wheels are made of wood.
They wear out quickly.
To make them last longer
a metal strip is fitted round
the rim.

The tyres of buses, lorries and cars are made of steel and thick rubber.
The steel gives the tyre its shape and makes it strong.

When you blow up a balloon
the rubber feels hard
because the balloon
is packed with air.
When a tyre is fitted to a
wheel air is pumped into it
to make it hard.

Rubber tyres have a pattern called a tread.
The tread helps the tyre to grip the road.

Some wheels need a special kind of tread.
The pattern of this tread helps the tractor to move on soft and muddy earth.

Sometimes even the wheels
of a tractor can get stuck.
The wheels on this earthmover
turn inside a track.
They run on their own road!

Sometimes, when the roads are covered with ice and snow, chains are fitted around tyres.
The chains grip the icy road and the wheels turn without slipping.

Where else do you find wheels?
There are wheels on aircraft…

and on caravans and
motorcycles.

There are wheels on shoes and on suitcases.

Chairs can also have wheels.

Some wheels don't have a tyre or flat rim. How does this kind of wheel keep the train on the track?

How many wheels can you find in this picture?

This wheel has teeth
cut around the rim.
It is called a cog wheel.

The teeth in one cog wheel fit into the teeth of the cog wheel next to it. When the first wheel turns the next wheel turns too.

Where can you find cog wheels like this? What happens when the cog wheels turn?

This is a water wheel.
When water falls on the wheel
the wheel turns.
The turning wheel
drives machinery
inside the mill.

Wheels are used to
steer buses and boats...

and to have fun.

Wheels are used in many
different ways.
What would life be like
without wheels?

About this book

All books which are specially prepared for young children are
written to meet the interest of the age group at which they are
directed. This may mean presenting an idea in a humorous or
unconventional way so that ideas which hitherto have been
grasped somewhat hazily are given sharper focus. The books in
this series aim to bring into focus some of the elements of life and
living which we as adults tend to take for granted.

This book develops and explores an idea using simple text and
thought-provoking photographs. The words will encourage
questioning and discussion – whether they are read by adult or
child. Children enjoy having information books read to them just
as much as stories and poetry. The younger child may ignore the
written words … pictures play an important part in learning,
particularly if they encourage talk and visual discrimination.

Young children acquire much information in an incidental, almost
random fashion. Indeed, they learn much just by being alive! The
adult who uses books like this one needs to be sympathetic and
understanding of the the young child's intellectual development.
It offers a particular way of looking, an approach to questioning
which will result in talk, rather than 'correct' one word answers.

Henry Pluckrose